India: Striding Or Colliding Into The Next Millennium?

CSC 1998

Subject Area – Topical Issues

EXECUTIVE SUMMARY

Title: INDIA: STRIDING OR COLLIDING INTO THE NEXT MILLENNIUM?

Author: Major Douglas Hardison, United States Marine Corps

Thesis: Solving the Asian security equation and preventing intra regional conflict will pose great difficulties for US policy makers in the next century. Most forecasts portray China as the unchallenged winner both economically, politically and militarily. However, in the 21st century, Chinese regional dominance will be challenged by India. India cannot afford to maintain a lower tier status within Asia without risking disintegration of its internal union. As a potential hegemon and imperial rival to Chinese power within Asia, India's challenge could pose a threat to Asian stability in the coming century.

Discussion: India represents the world's largest democratic nation uniquely situated within the Indian Ocean. Traditionally, the US has considered India a strategic backwater. With an ethnically diverse and religiously split population, limited physical resources, and a large segment of the population in poverty, Indian strategists' primary concern is internal unity. Furthermore, Indian strategists perceive sustained economic development as the adhesive for managing the ethnic, historical and political forces that are fragmenting the Indian Union. Economic expansion has begun, but its full potential has been hampered by the splintering of India's core political organizations as well as traditionalists who want to retain centralized control over the economy.

Economic expansion relates directly to India's strategy of enhancing its regional and international position, national security and strategic influence. From the Indian perspective, the status quo will not provide for long term national strength which equates to national unity. As India struggles to enhance its political and economic position, historical conflicts with Pakistan and China, combined with a suspicion concerning US policy in South Asia, counter Indian aims for sub regional dominance and greater regional prominence. In its efforts to gain greater influence, India has pursued a moderately aggressive nuclear and missile program, and the Indian military denotes a pattern of increased capabilities with a desire for power projection through aviation and naval procurements. However, the immaturity of the strategic planning process within the Indian government adds a destabilizing variable to the equation as Indian planners try to link strategic actions to objectives without a clear sense of the consequences.

Although Indian strategists recognize Pakistan as the most immediate threat to security, India planners feel that they have ample justification to be concerned about China's long-term strategic intentions. Indian strategists are alarmed by Chinese support for Pakistan in the form of M-11 missiles, ring magnets for nuclear research, and general military equipment. Amplifying Indian concerns of encroachment are Chinese military relations with Burma. China's vital interests relate directly to its overriding priority for economic development which includes access to Southeast Asian markets. Dr. Ronald Montaperto from the Institute for National Strategic Studies at the National Defense University

i

comments that "the Indian interface with China in Southeast Asia may well mark a major fault line within the Asia Pacific region as two large and populous nations seek to achieve what each considers to be vital national interests."

Conclusion(s) or Recommendation(s): Interpreting the variables that will affect India's future external relations against the backdrop of expanding Chinese interests will reveal the potential for intra regional conflict as the US makes policy within the parameters of the 21st century Asian security equation.

CONTENTS

INDIA: STRIDING OR COLLIDING INTO THE NEXT MILLENNIUM?

TRANSITIONING TO MULTIPOLAR POLITICS

The United States' economic health has become increasingly dependent upon those economies that lie along the Pacific Ocean, Indian Ocean and Persian Gulf littoral. This observation directly contrasts normal US fixation on European issues. Speaking before a group of Asian scholars and businessmen, US Defense Secretary William Cohen recognized the critical importance of this region when he noted, "The Mediterranean is the ocean of the past. The Atlantic is the ocean of the present. And the Pacific is the ocean of the future."[1] However, defining international relationships in Asia is a bedeviling process. The implosion of the Soviet Union in 1991 seemed to offer the US a clear picture of its strength, capabilities and unlimited potential within the world. Instead, the disintegration of the Soviet Union opened a Pandora's box of uncertainty for the US, especially in Asia. The distinction between friend and foe became blurred as the world order shifted from an ideological and common security stance to economic-based competition. This has created a geopolitical situation in Asia that does not have direct and definable solutions. Comprehending the shape of this new geopolitical environment requires a shift from bipolar political thinking to multipolar thought processes.

The dynamics of the US and USSR confrontation lent itself to a certain predictability. Regional politics were a zero sum game, and there was a clearly defined political fence.

---

[1] Secretary William S. Cohen, US Secretary of Defense remarks during an Asia Society conference, 6/11/97, downloaded from DefenseLINK News (Quantico, VA: Erols), 24 November 1997.

Multipolar politics are best analogous to pre-World War I Europe during the Balkan Wars of 1912-1913. As the Turkish empire receded, the region was marked with shifting alliances and fast paced diplomatic efforts as the Great Powers of Europe labored for peace within this historically unstable region. A peaceful settlement within this multipolar environment was difficult to achieve because of the necessity to negotiate within the interests of all the parties involved.[2] This complexity is evident in Asia today as the US maneuvers politically, economically, and militarily to best position itself to reap the benefits of expanding markets and economies.

Purpose

"Asia's economic promise depends greatly upon regional security."[3] Maintaining stability within Asia is paramount for US interests. In the future, dwindling resources and access to markets will stress political relationships. These developments will likely increase the potential for intra-regional conflict. The focus of US interest has been predominantly on US-China relations with attention fixed on the large and undeveloped China "market." This China-centric view has emerged because of the general belief that China will transition to a super power early in the next century. But the world will not likely fall back into the binary system that emerged after World War II. This is apparent for four reasons. China faces fierce economic competition from all its Asian neighbors as well as the rest of the world. Strategically, China is not focused globally but regionally.[4] Third, US economic and military power is not static and will most likely decrease against strengthening European and

---

2   Robert Leonhard, *The Art of Maneuver*, (Novato, CA: Presidio Press, 1991), 227.

3   Gen Charles C. Krulak, Commandant of the Marine Corps, "Protecting the Asian Promise," *Strategic Review* 24, no. 3 (Summer 1996): 9.

4   James L. Lacy, *Cautious Peace: Strategy and Circumstance in Asia-Pacific Security*, Monograph No. P-3108, Institute for Defense Analyses (Alexandria, VA: July 1995), 78.

East Asian countries. Finally, Chinese regional dominance will be challenged by India. "India is the one other potential hegemon and imperial rival to Chinese power within the greater region."[5] In an evolving multipolar world, this observation from James Lacy of the Institute of Defense Analyses, brings a substantial variable to the Asian security equation.

India represents the world's largest democratic nation uniquely situated within the Indian Ocean. Traditionally, the US has considered India a strategic backwater. This mindset has been slow to change. With a diverse and religiously split population, limited physical resources, and a large segment of the population in poverty, India displays all the traditional symptoms of a problematic third world country. However, since independence in 1947, India has pursued a moderately aggressive military development program and in 1974 detonated a nuclear device. The social and political indicators are deceptive. On one side, India's extensive technical base and growing middle class lead to a perception that India will mature into a fully integrated developed nation, but other indicators show a fragmented democracy held together by common external threats. Historical conflicts with Pakistan and China, combined with a suspicion concerning US policy in the Persian Gulf and South Asia, make Indian intentions difficult to anticipate. Internally, Indian society is facing monumental changes as it transitions from an agrarian economy to a more industrialized economy. Interpreting the variables that will affect India's future external relations against the backdrop of expanding Chinese interests will reveal the potential for intra-regional conflict as the US makes policy within the parameters of the 21st century Asian security equation.

_____

5   Lacy, 86.

Scope

Mechanisms that underlie the actions of a society do not follow linear relationships. If this was the case, political scientists or researchers could "deal with linear relationships -- relationships that are strictly proportional and therefore expressible as lines on a graph" and make clear and simple predictions concerning the system's behavior.[6] A dynamic, interactive society makes predicting the intentions or progress of that society a frustrating effort.   However, societies do develop patterns as they interact, develop and adapt within a regional or global system.[7]   Societal patterns offer the observer a method of anticipating rather than predicting future developments based on trends and other key indicators. Understanding these patterns or trends is not based on the composition or structure of components but is related to the activity of the components.[8] This activity can be equated to behavior.

With behavior as the focus, the first chapter will frame the Indian thought process as it relates to national strategy. The construct of Indian national strategy is embedded in historical, political and economic factors. This constitutes the foundation for how India comprehends and behaves regionally and globally. The second chapter will survey India's armed forces and nuclear program. This addresses capabilities as a baseline but concentrates on the trends and direction of the Indian military in the future. The last chapter assesses Indian relationships with Pakistan, the US, and China through a discussion of key issues that denote emerging and recognizable patterns for future relations. With a framework erected,

---

[6]   COL Glenn M. Harned, USA, *The Complexity of War: The Application of Nonlinear Science to Military Science*, Monograph, Marine Corps War College (Quantico, VA: June 1995), 22.

[7]   Roger Lewin, *Complexity, Life at the Edge of Chaos* (New York: Collier Books, 1992), 15.

[8]   Mitchell M. Waldrop, *Complexity: The Emerging Science at the Edge of Order and Chaos* (New York: Simon and Schuster, 1992), 292.

Indian behavior patterns as they relate to national perceptions, future military capabilities, and changing foreign relations will become more visible. These conclusions will frame India's potential role within this charged and dynamic region of the world.

CHAPTER ONE

THE WORLD ACCORDING TO INDIA

1.1 India's Strategic Priority

"India's most pressing strategic security concern is its own internal unity."[9] These words echoed from RAND strategist George Tanham in his "Indian Strategic Thought: An Interpretive Essay" categorize the most serious problem Indian nationalists face. As politicians and Indian strategists voice concern about the future of India, basic issues of Indian national security become discernible. Supported by historical, political and economic evidence, these concerns will further define future behavior patterns relating to external interaction. These patterns relate to India's overarching concern for internal security and political dominance within the subcontinent.

1.2 A Historical Perspective

The idea of an Indian "state" is a recent phenomenon. India has been a collection of societies and cultures much longer than it has been a unified nation. "The country has 14 different [official] languages, 24 languages spoken by a million or more people, and hundreds of lesser languages and dialects."[10] The national language is Hindi; however, only a third of the country can speak the language. Burdened with ethnic and religious struggles that predate Indian independence and the partition of Pakistan, Hindu-Moslem tensions and Sikh nationalism in Punjab are just two examples of the numerous influences that act against

---

9   George K. Tanham, *Indian Strategic Thought: An Interpretive Essay*, no. R-4207-USDP (Santa Monica, CA: The Rand Corp., 1992), 24.

10   COL Floyd L. Perry, USA, *The Future of U.S. - India Relations*, Monograph, U.S. Army War College (Carlisle Barracks, PA: 1991), 15.

1

the union of India. Understanding this dichotomy of Indian nationalism versus ethnic regionalism underscores Indian strategists' primary fear of internal disorder.

Largely contributing to ethnic diversity, the geography of the Indian subcontinent led to the development of a number of independent kingdoms and principalities, separated by natural internal barriers like mountains and rivers. Over time, strategic concerns became differentiated by region. Furthermore, external barriers played more of a role keeping Indians inside the subcontinent rather than keeping foreign aggressors out. A succession of Central Asian invaders entered the subcontinent from mountain passes located in present day Afghanistan and Pakistan. This history of invasion from land armies has given the northern region a strong strategic land orientation as well as cultural influences from numerous invaders. To the South, the original Dravidian language and culture remained relatively untouched as land invaders generally remained in the North.[11] However, the southern region, marked by an expansive coastline, proved to be an ineffective barrier to a succession of European colonizers including the Dutch, Portuguese, French and British.

The geographical differences that made the northern region the "heartland of India" tended to fragment the development of the southern region and allow its domination by the North.[12] This has resulted in southerners resenting northern dominance and focusing strategically towards the sea. However, a common pattern throughout the subcontinent's diverse development was a perception of external insecurity highlighted by hyper-regionalism. This feeling of insecurity was the realization that the subcontinent's extensive natural barriers were not impermeable and that regional differences invited foreign aggression.

The Indian union, during its few periods of existence, has been more an assortment of independent states held together by force than joined for the common good. The

---

[11]   Tanham, 3.

[12]   Tanham, 6.

Mauryan, Moghul and British empires all exercised force to maintain the integrity of their empires. Only through British colonial "nationalization" efforts did Indian nationalists realize their aspiration of an independent India. Many areas within India still require the need for military force to maintain the union. Regional dissidence within Kashmir, Punjab, and the Northeast territories illustrates the persistent "problem" New Delhi faces as the government struggles to keep ethnic separatism contained. Documented by Amnesty International and Asiawatch, large scale human rights abuses conducted by Indian security forces appear to run counter to the aims of a democratic government.[13] However, these measures are defended by the government of Indian (GOI) as legitimate and necessary within the context of societal order and national unity.

1.3 *Politically Splintered*

Paralleling India's "independent-minded" ethnic groups, the country's core political organizations have undergone extensive fragmentation. A steady decline of the Congress party's power coupled with the growing politicization of numerous social groups has created an indistinguishable political picture. After single party domination for fifty years, the elections in 1996 produced no clear majority. The decline of the dominant Congress party began in 1967 when the party almost lost its parliamentary majority and was accelerated when Indira Gandhi (Nehru's daughter) took control of the party in 1969. This reflected a change from the centralized rule that New Delhi had exercised since before independence to a power base generated regionally. Indira Gandhi was able to maintain popular support by reaching down to grass root levels and appealing to the lower and poorer castes. As certain party leaders with their own power bases revolted against populist politics, the party effectively split. This created two outcomes. First, Indira Gandhi's Congress (I) party

---

13   Barbara Leitch LePoer, *India - US Relations*, No. 93097, downloaded from the Congressional Research Service Issue Brief: Foreign Affairs and National Defense Division (Quantico, VA: Erols), 9 December 1996, 10.

3

"never acquired the hallmarks of an organized party."[14] Second, the disenfranchised opposition organized and competed with the new Congress (I) party at the same regional level as Indira Gandhi. The power of this opposition movement grew for the next two decades and by the mid-1970's was successfully competing against the Congress (I) party. Indira Gandhi, reacting to the strength of the opposition, instituted "Emergency" powers between 1975-1977. Following the return to "normal" political processes, opposition parties briefly established a tenuous majority government between 1977-1980.

In the early 1980's, Indira Gandhi began to mobilize support around Hindu issues as her populist support began to wane. This was the first time since the 1940's that religious themes had been used in a national election.[15] Her assassination in 1984 vaulted the Congress (I) party to victory through her son Rajiv. His assassination in 1991 gave the Congress (I) party five more years of control, but the ability of the Congress (I) party to maintain a dominating position ended with the loss of the political icon that the Nehru family represented.

The peripheral parties that have emerged in the mid-1990's connote a trend in Indian politics to broadened representation and regional politics. These groups have taken advantage of the populist and religious themes that Indira Gandhi generated. The United Front (UF) which took power in 1996 represents the party to the center of this group. Composed of a loose coalition of regional and centrist parties, the UF focuses on the decentralization of government, support for agriculture and tempered politics of

---

[14]   Atul Kohli, "Can the Periphery Control the Center? Indian Politics at the Crossroads," *The Washington Quarterly* 19, no. 4 (Autumn 1996): 116.

[15]   Kohli, 117.

redistribution.[16] The Communist party of India (CPM) lies to the left of the political spectrum. The CPM only holds power in the two states of West Bengal and Kerala, and it has a good record of pragmatic leadership. However, the influence of the CPM has not spread or increased.

The most dramatic increase in political power in recent years has been the Bharatiya Janata Party (BJP). Its political power is concentrated mostly in north-central and north-western India where Mohgul rule was the most pronounced (and Moslem minorities are greatest), and it holds approximately 20 percent of the national electorate as of 1996.[17] The evolution of this party originated before independence as a form of Hindu nationalism. The pre-independence movement was a response to fears that the central government through British control was subjugating the Hindu majority through the extension of preferential treatment to Muslims and lower castes. The BJP is a translation of this movement responding to what it perceives as the same discrimination against the Hindu majority with the extension of preferential treatment in the form of equal opportunity and affirmative action policies to the lower levels of Indian society. However, Hinduism is a highly amorphous and polytheist religious tradition, and attempts at defining an orthodox position have not been successful enough to increase its share of the vote since 1991.[18] Ultimately, the BJP, UF, and CPM all represent the growing trend within Indian politics to regional issues, decentralization of power and opposition to centralized rule characterized by the Congress (I) party.

Although the three largest political parties (Congress [I] party, BJP and UF) have relatively diverse positions, each party has taken a centrist and consensus building approach

---

[16]   Kohli, 121.

[17]   Kohli, 125.

[18]   Kohli, 125.

to government when in power.[19] Essential differences do exist: a nationalist oriented BJP which threatens India's minorities; a Congress (I) party focused on continued economic liberalization; and the UF concentrating on its social democratic traditions. Central rule from New Delhi through strong personalities like Indira and Rajiv Gandhi has been superseded by growing regional parties. This trend in Indian politics is more the norm for Indian civilization and reflects the extreme regional diversity within India. However, implementing a coherent national policy depends on the development of a relatively unified power base. Political observers have characterized recent Indian governments as weak and inactive.[20] However, as one coalition government after another struggles to develop initiatives and reform strategies, the "political gusts" will continue to produce a multitude of "inconsistent policies" that bewilder observers both in and outside of India.[21]

1.4 Economic Glue

Indian strategists perceive sustained economic development as the adhesive for managing the ethnic, historical, and political forces that work to fragment the Indian union. New Delhi, not unlike other Asian capitals, believes that "the health and resilience of the Indian political system and, in a larger sense, of Indian society" is directly proportional to its economic strength.[22] From a post-Cold War viewpoint, economic strength has become the "new" measure that Indian planners use to define India's political position both regionally and globally. As a direct corollary, continued economic development also provides the necessary resources to modernize India's defense forces. From this perspective, a discussion

---

[19]   Kohli, 126.

[20]   Kohli, 127.

[21]   Kenneth J. Cooper, "With Door to Economy Ajar, India Can't Stop Shivering", *Washington Post,* 19 September 1997, Sec. A16.

[22]   Dr. Ronald N. Montaperto, *Emerging Dynamics of Indian Policy: A View from the United States*, a discussion paper presented at the 1997 India Symposium sponsored by the National Defense University at Ft. McNair, Washington, D.C. on 3 December 1997, 2.

of India's economic development and prognosis will uncover the problems associated with India's strategic concerns.

At independence, Indian leaders consolidated central power by directing agricultural and industrial development. This was a method of maintaining internal security while raising India's standard of living. Facing repeated food shortages in the 1960's, the Indian government began a program to enhance crop production called the "green revolution."[23] With the implementation of modern agricultural methods like fertilizers, expanded irrigation techniques, and improved strains of rice and wheat, agricultural output improved dramatically. However, emphasis was placed on increasing agricultural output by technical means rather than countering the massive inequalities among the rural population. This would bring to the forefront issues like water and property rights along with caste and privilege issues.[24] The green revolution has reached its technical limits. This has serious implications for a population that will reach one billion sometime in the early 21st century. The agricultural sector employs over half of the population, and if agricultural activity stagnates, the drag on the economy will be serious. The problems associated with liberalizing agricultural policies within India lies with fragmented regional politics, over-regulation and the inertia of a large bureaucracy. The paradox is that "successful Asian economies [have] built their rapid growth around success in the farming sector."[25] China's emergence as an economic powerhouse originated with agricultural reforms instituted in 1978. Increased agricultural income created an increased demand for manufactured products

---

[23]   Dennis Kux, *India and the United States: Estranged Democracies 1941-1991* (Washington, DC: National Defense University Press, 1993), 242.

[24]   Paul Kennedy, *Preparing For The Twenty-First Century* (New York: Vintage Books, 1994), 171.

[25]   Ramesh Thakur, *The Politics and Economics of India's Foreign Policy* (New York: St. Martin's Press, 1994), 268.

which had an upward spiraling effect on labor and material resources within China. If India is to parallel this success, it will have to tackle these political and social issues.

India's answer to its economic problems was a policy of trade and industrial liberalization. Enacted in 1991, this was an abrupt change from an economy that relied on centralized direction, industrial subsidies, high tariffs, import restrictions and other protectionist policies. However, with the collapse of the Soviet Union, India's largest trading partner, and "years of budgetary indiscipline by successive governments," India's economy was on the brink.[26] By 1990, 410 million Indians as compared to 120 million Chinese were under the poverty line. This line is defined by an affordable, nutritionally adequate diet and the provision of essential non-food requirements.[27] A rapidly deteriorating situation resulted in an opportunity for Prime Minister P.V. Narasimha Rao and Finance Minister Manmohan Singh to reverse the protectionist policies that had been created in the 1950's. Eliminating the industrial licensing system, reducing tariff and income taxes, permitting foreign investment in the stock market and other sweeping market reforms encouraged foreign investment and trade. Additionally, economic growth rates which fell below 1 percent in 1991-92, rebounded to 5 percent and 4 1/2 percent the following two years. In 1995-96, growth rates had risen to 6.7 percent while inflation had fallen to 7-8 percent from 11 percent.[28] This economic reversal has given confidence to Indian and foreign investors alike. A combination of a large middle class of 150 million, a substantial professional class, and preliminary pro-business policies makes India appear a lucrative market.[29]

---

[26]   Thakur, 262.

[27]   Thakur 264.

[28]   Francine Frankel, "Indo-U.S. Relations: The Future is Now," *The Washington Quarterly* 19, no. 4 (Autumn 1996): 132.

[29]   Thakur, 286.

However, the path for Indian economic development is tenuous. The cancellation of the Enron $2.8 billion Dhabol power project and the temporary closure of Kentucky Fried Chicken restaurants in Delhi and Bangalore reflects India's hostility and suspicion towards foreign companies that continue from the British colonial era.[30] Bureaucratic red tape within India is still prolific, and corruption and bribery are thoroughly institutionalized within the country. Inflexible labor laws make shedding excess labor costly while discouraging industrial expansion. These characteristics are unproductive and will dampen future economic prospects. Further, when foreign direct investment rates are compared, India at $1 billion (1995 data) lags far behind countries like China and Indonesia with foreign investment at $22 billion and $18 billion respectively.[31] Yet, it is these disparities in foreign direct investment that reflect the intense economic competition emerging in Asia. Although the door has been opened for India, the conditions for accelerated growth as experienced by the "Tigers" of the Pacific Rim are not fully in place with expanded decentralization measures and agricultural liberalization .

Economically, India faces an extreme contest between those traditional policy makers who want to retain centralized control of the economy and reformers who see decentralized control and a free market economy as a means to induce rapid growth. India's success will be measured by its participation in the Asian and global economy. This struggle is evident in political circles on the eve of the February 1998 National elections. Mr. Manmohan Singh, who is credited as the architect of India's 1991 economic reforms, is likely to be the Congress (I) party's choice for leader in the parliament in a UF and Congress (I) party bid against the

---

30   John Stremlau, "Dateline Bangalore: Third World Technopolis," *Foreign Policy* no. 102 (Spring 1996): 162.

31   James C. Clad, "India in 1996: Steady as She Goes," *The Washington Quarterly* 19, no. 4 (Autumn 1996): 108.

BJP.[32]   However, even if successful, Mr. Singh faces a pitched battle against numerous forces that will continue to threaten India's efforts to maintain its economic momentum.

1.5 Strategic Interests

Economic development relates directly to India's strategy of enhancing its regional and international position, national security and strategic influence.[33] From the Indian perspective, the status quo will not provide for long term national strength which equates to national unity. However, economic reform requires strong leadership and a coherent national strategy which does not seem likely in the near term.

Within a greater context, Indian strategists view the entire subcontinent as India's strategic domain. With the exception of Pakistan, no country within the South Asia subregion poses a threat to India. Although separate states, all South Asian countries share a certain amount of cultural unity, history and many of the same problems, including ethnic separatism, dwindling resources, and burgeoning populations. However, tension exists between India and its neighbors. The tensions for these smaller nations revolve around political insecurity and India's immense size. Measures like the South Asian Association for Regional Cooperation (SAARC) and the recently created SAARC Preferential Trading Arrangement (SAPTA) have generated marginal optimism concerning economic expansion in South Asia.[34] However, the issues in these forums revolve around domestic and economic policies of free trade and have not delved into the "toughest barrier" to subregional

---

32   "Sonia's Choice," *The Economist,* 31 January 1998, 43.

33   Montaperto, 2.

34   Kishore C. Dash, "The Political Economy of Regional Cooperation in South Asia," *Pacific Affairs* 69, no. 2 (Summer 1996): 185.

free trade: "the psychological line between India and Pakistan."[35] The historic animosities that exist between these two states tugs against the multinational effort to generate South Asian economic expansion while India's security policies have created a cautious attitude among South Asian nations regarding Indian intentions.

Labeled the "Indira Doctrine," Indians liken this national security doctrine to the United States Monroe Doctrine.[36] Taking its roots from British-era treaties that allowed the British Government of India to conduct foreign and extra-regional defensive policies for nations and princely states within the subcontinent, modern India has created similar treaties with some of its subcontinental neighbors. Examples of this strategic disposition include the 1988 military intervention in the Maldives and numerous occasions of political and economic pressure applied to nations like Nepal and Bhutan. Additionally, India's bitter denouncements against US support for Pakistan during the Cold War was a direct expression of this security mind-set.

The "Indira Doctrine" expanded to include the Indian Ocean which India perceives as its natural maritime domain. This maritime interest originates from fears generated by British colonial domination that foreign powers could threaten Indian interests by establishing seaborne ties with some of India's smaller neighbors. Statements by Admiral S.N. Kohli about the US deployment of a carrier battle group to the Bay of Bengal during India's 1971 intervention in East Pakistan typify this insecurity:

> It was a clear attempt by the US to divert Indian forces and to frighten us and dissuade us from proceeding with our course of action. The scenario was the same - one large power from across the sea with its superior naval forces coming to the aid of a country

---

35   Gautam Adhikari, *Sleeping with the Enemy: Problems of Economic Security in South Asia*, a discussion paper presented at the 1997 India Symposium sponsored by the National Defense University at Ft. McNair, Washington, D.C. on 3 December 1997, 5.

36   Tanham, 29.

in South Asia against another - only the timing was some centuries later. It was a blatant attempt on the part of the US to indulge in an act of 'gunboat diplomacy'.[37] This action inflamed Indian nationalists, and "[e]ven today, U.S. diplomats visiting India are reminded of this incident."[38] Indian elites perceive their national security interests as the subregion's first priority, and rationalizing this perception, they believe the benefits of this Indian generated security blanket benefits all states within the subcontinent.

Recently, former Prime Minister Gujral has been credited with developing a new policy of "neighborly relations" which strives to reduce tensions with Pakistan and improve relations with India's other neighbors.[39] This policy does not necessarily negate the "Indira Doctrine" as much as realize the economic necessity to consolidate India's position within South Asia and gain a greater lattitude to pursue larger economic objectives in the rest of Asia and globally. However, a statement by the former executive editor of the *Times of India*, Mr. Gautam Adhikari, describes these efforts against the probability of success in a typically Indian manner: "Experience shows that the announced desires of South Asian political leaders and their real movements toward purposeful action usually betray a disparity over time."[40]

A history of invasion combined with a British-generated sensitivity to being treated as inferior has created a fiercely protective attitude concerning what India perceives as its domain. India's behavior often appears as an overreaction to events as the national

---

[37] Adm. S.N. Kohli, PVSM, AVSM, "The geopolitical and strategic considerations that necessitate the expansion and modernization of the Indian Navy," *Indian Defence Review* 2 (January 1989): 37.

[38] "Exploring U.S. Missile Defense Requirements in 2010: What are the Policy and Technology Challenges?," Institute for Foreign Policy Analyses Inc., April 1997, downloaded from the Federation of American Scientists: Missile Defense Monitor (Quantico, VA: Erols), 15 September 1997, Chap 4 pg 8.

[39] Montaperto, 5.

[40] Adhikari, 8.

government struggles to demonstrate its subregional and internal dominance. However, this behavior conflicts with trends toward fragmenting central power and economic policies of liberalization. Indian elites face a lose-lose situation. Expanding economic development both internally and within the subregion will mean loosening India's political grasp. This effort is paramount if India and its neighbors are to graduate to a higher economic level and raise the standard of living for their impoverished populations. However, maintaining an internal union and simultaneuously influencing South Asia requires exercising strong leadership from New Delhi. The GOI gives few signs of this sort of stability. These factors have no equilibrium and will teeter on their interaction within the greater arena of international relations.

CHAPTER TWO

BRANDISHING THE SWORD?

2.1 Providing the Means

Security interests are tempered by the means used to achieve them. While India would like to reduce the level of defense spending, it fears both external attack and internal disorder that mandate high levels of defense appropriations. Historically, the Indian armed forces never developed an expansionist tradition. However, this inclination is changing as India's military modernizes, incorporates lessons from its conflicts with Pakistan and China and exploits ideas gained by the US experience during the Persian Gulf War.[41] India's nuclear and missile programs also provide signals of India's desire to become a recognized regional if not global power. An examination of these and other military trends will provide a reference and direction for India's military capability in 21st century Asia.

2.2 Matching the Threat

India's most immediate external threat lies on its border with Pakistan. This has made the Army, with over one half of India's defense budget, the dominant service. Interestingly, while one third of the military continually faces the Pakistani border, India maintains nearly 20 percent of its land forces in a counter-insurgency role in troubled regions like Kashmir and Nagaland.[42] Equipped with a combination of former Soviet Union and indigenously

---

[41] For an excellent example of an Indian analysis and critique of the US conduct of the Persian Gulf War refer to *War in the Gulf: Lessons for the Third World* by BrigGen V.K. Nair, VSM (Ret.), published by Lancer Int., New Delhi, 1991.

[42] Col Nancy Anderson, USMC, and Jed Snyder, "India and Pakistan," Chapter 10 in *Strategic Assessment 1997: Flashpoints and Force Structure*, eds. Hans A. Binnendijk and Patrick Clawson, Institute for National Strategic Studies (Washington DC: Ft. McNair, 1997), 123.

developed military hardware, India's military strength in personnel has declined in numbers from a peak strength during the 1970's of 1.2 million to just over 1 million in 1998. The Army's emphasis has been placed on joint military operations at the operational level of war, the mechanization of the Indian Army, and integration of civilian infrastructure to support military operations through massive exercises like Brass Tacks (Pakistani scenario) and Checker Board (Chinese scenario) during the late 1980's.[43] Exercise Brass Board was to be the culmination exercise to demonstrate India's ability to fight a two-front war. Because of the crisis created with the Pakistanis and Chinese with the two previous exercises and the provocative nature of the two-front exercise, the Indian government opted to cancel the event. However, these exercises and force modernization programs indicate Indian armed forces are working towards a more active defense with some offensive capability.

This process is apparent in an operational context as well. Before 1971, the Indian armed forces tended to concentrate massive quantities of men and material in a systematic and static battle doctrine.[44] The 1971 war with Pakistan marked a change from this thought pattern as India conducted this short war through maneuver and localized superiority. From a strategic perspective, India maneuvered to preempt China from entering the conflict by entering into the 1971 Indo-Soviet Friendship Treaty prior to the conflict. At lower levels, India's liaison with insurgent forces of East Pakistan reduced Pakistani capabilities to counter an Indian invasion. India's peacekeeping operation in Sri Lanka, although widely hailed as a military failure, deployed four infantry divisions and appoximately five independent brigades

---

[43]   Kanti P. Bajpai and others, *BrassTacks and Beyond* (New Delhi: Manohar Pub., 1995), 11.

[44]   MAJ Robert D. Cox, USA, *India and the Operational Art of War,* Monograph, U.S. Army Command and General Staff College, School of Advanced Military Studies (Ft. Leavenworth, KS: 1991), 12.

to counter the civil unrest in this country.[45] Other operations, like the Maldives action in 1988, also demonstrate India's efforts to develop a force projection capability. With short notice, India deployed approximately 3000 soldiers almost 350 miles from the Indian coastline to successfully counter a coup attempt in the Maldives.[46]

2.3 Modernization

An economic downturn in 1991 and subsequent emphasis on economic liberalization has put a substantial burden on the Indian armed forces in their effort to modernize the force. Modernization programs have been scaled back or shelved through most of the 1990's. The modernization plan for the Indian Air Force (IAF) is a prominent example of India's difficulties. Defense planners had developed a plan in the 1980's for 54 quality squadrons by the year 2000.[47] This plan stalled in the face of budget shortfalls, and India is in a quandary as it struggles to maintain the IAF composed of 43 squadrons of former Soviet, French and British aircraft. Future plans envision a smaller air force composed of an indigenous built aircraft called the Light Combat Aircraft (LCA), but the program has been hampered by delays and cost overruns. However, the disintegration of the Soviet Union and the difficulties in negotiating and enforcing military contracts with the Commonwealth of Independent States has prompted the Indian government to require the Defence ministry to promote 70 percent of the ministry's annual budget to domestic acquisitions.[48] Until the LCA is introduced, the IAF must decide to upgrade its large inventory of MIG-21's or

---

[45]   MAJ James D. Scudieri, *The Indian Peace-Keeping Force in Sri Lanka, 1987-90*, Monograph, School of Advanced Military Studies, US Army Command and General Staff College (Ft. Leavenworth, KS: December 1994), 52.

[46]   Cox, 40.

[47]   Dr. D. Shridhar, "Testing Times Ahead for Indian Air Force," *Asia-Pacific Defence Reporter*, September-October, 1996, 13.

[48]Shridhar, 13.

acquire the Su30. Neither option is attractive because of the cost and the continued dependence on outside sources for military support, and until the Indian economy is stronger, it is unlikely that the Ministry of Defense will enjoy any great increases in its budget.

While the economic downturn of 1991-92 had a severe impact on the overall military budget, the Indian Navy's budget within this period surprisingly grew four percent adjusted for inflation.[49] This increase is significant because it demonstrates India's growing perception of itself as a maritime power within the Indian Ocean, and India's increasing trend away from a coastal navy to a navy capable of sea control and power projection. Questionable Chinese activities vis-a-vis Taiwan in the South China Sea and China's alignment with Burma, which potentially offers China naval bases bordering the Indian Ocean, combined with growing regional navies within the Association of South East Asian Nations (ASEAN) only heighten Indian sensitivities concerning its naval disposition and capabilities to counter these maritime trends.[50] Table one provides a naval order of battle for India, China, and Japan. Although the table illustrates India's relative weakness in capital platforms, it does capture the emphasis that India places for a power projection capability in the form of a carrier. The Indian Navy, recently retiring its first carrier, has one remaining vertical take-off (VSTOL) aircraft carrier that it acquired from Great Britain. While India maintains a smaller relative naval force when compared to China and Japan, its carrier and assortment of destroyers, frigates, submarines, and maritime aircraft that support the

---

49   LT William J. Nault, USN, *The Strategic Impact Upon the United States of Future Naval Rivalries in South and Southeast Asia,* Monograph, Naval Postgraduate School (Monterey, CA: December 1992), 80.

50   Nault, 79.

Armed Forces	Personnel	Armored Divisions	RAPID Divisions
India	1,145,000	3.00	4.00
Pakistan	587,000	2.00	0.00

Table 1. Derived from *The Military Balance 1997/1998.* Edited by Col Terence Taylor and published by Oxford University for the International Institute for Strategic Studies.

fleet give India a viable capability to project combat power. Additionally, a comparison of platforms fails to portray India's ability to project naval power from its shores and island territories by taking advantage of its central geographic disposition within the Indian ocean.

2.4 Status

Status and symbolism are important in Indian society as reflected by societal beliefs best illustrated by the caste system. The proximity of the Strait of Hormuz and the Straits of Malacca, critical choke points along sea lines of communication, only accent India's feelings of geostrategic importance. With the country's sheer physical size, large population, and position within the Indian Ocean, Indian leaders have always maintained India's regional and global importance.[51] Yet gaining recognition of this status has been a frustrating effort. The indignation that Indian political elites voice at not receiving recognition as a world power and a permanent position within the United Nations (UN) Security Council typifies this sensitivity towards unequal standing in international affairs. Compounding their frustrations, Indian elites consider their blue water navy, large army and other military trappings representative of great power status which has not been properly recognized. [52] This desire for status often puts the Indian defense planner in a poor position to explain

---

[51]   Kux, 449.

[52]   Tanham, 60.

18

India's developmental efforts for a number of clearly offensive weapon systems such as nuclear submarines or submarine launched cruise missiles (*Sagarika*) within the context of an articulated mission.[53] Indian claims for peaceful intentions run against its efforts to gain clearly offensive weapon systems.

The purest examples of this focus on status and symbols are India's nuclear and missile programs. A "peaceful" nuclear explosion in 1974 and extensive nuclear development combined with the recent "demonstration" of the *Agni* Inter-Regional Ballistic Missile (IRBM) exemplifies India's tendencies toward offensive weapons systems. In one sense India has the best of both worlds. By demonstrating a "capability," India enjoys a certain strategic deterrence with both Pakistan and China. The *Agni* IRBM with a range of 1500 miles is a clear signal of India's nuclear strike potential to counter Chinese nuclear missiles deployed in Tibet. This signal is sent at a relatively cheap price because India does not have to build and deploy the missiles or the nuclear warheads. In addition, India enjoys a certain status as a nuclear club member without the associated costs of managing an arsenal. However, because India's missile and nuclear weapon programs are shrouded in mystery, the potential for miscommunication or misinterpretation of intentions has grave consequences.

2.5 *The Nuclear Question*

Nuclear threats from Pakistan's chief nuclear administrator Abdul Qadir Khan through an Indian journalist during the end of the Brass Tacks crisis in 1987 underscores the gravity of the situation.[54] Even though his remarks did not affect the outcome of the crisis, his comments outline the nuclear standoff that the South Asian region is facing. Another nuclear crisis occurred in 1990 when Indo-Pakistani relations again deteriorated. The

---

53   "Exploring U.S. Missile Defense Requirements in 2010: What are the Policy and Technology Challenges?," Chap 4 pg 9 and 25.

54   Bajpai, 39.

19

possibility of a Pakistani nuclear strike was seriously considered by the Indian government, and a task force was organized to study the implications of the threat and determine an appropriate response.[55]   Although the crisis ended after US mediation, that a task force was organized at all illustrated a disconnect within the Indian political-military strategic planning process. General Sundarji, who commanded the 1984 invasion of the Sikhs' Golden Temple in Amritsar and the 1987 intervention in Sri Lanka, put it more succinctly when he referred to Indian strategic planning institutions in a 1991 interview with the *Times of India*:

> In foreign and military policy one should expect a whole spectrum of scenarios from the sublime to the ridiculous and we should have all the possible answers worked out. That kind of discipline and institutional underpinning is just not there.[56]

With the overwhelming success of US forces in South West Asia in 1991 through a combination of overwhelming military power and political acumen, Indian strategists called for the establishment of a "National Policy Formulating body" and "National Security Agency" shortly after the Persian Gulf War.[57]   However, the recent creation of a National Security Council (NSC) has not taken final form, and the NSC has failed to function as it was envisioned.[58]   Given the historical animosities between India and her two primary opponents, India's failure to develop functioning planning institutions within a potentially

---

[55]   Amitabh Mattoo, "India's Nuclear Status Quo," *Survival: The IISS Quarterly* 38, no. 3 (Autumn 1996): 45.

[56]"Arms Control in South Asia," downloaded from the *Journal of the Federation of American Scientists: Public Interest Report* Vol. 47, March/April 1994 (Quantico, VA: Erols), 15 September 1997, 12.

[57]   BrigGen V.K. Nair, VSM (Ret.), *War in the Gulf: Lessons for the Third World* (New Delhi: Lancer Int., 1991), 221.

[58]   Gen K.V. Krishna Rao, PVSM (ret.), *Prepare or Perish: A Study of National Security* (New Delhi: Lancer Pub., 1991), 410.

nuclear tipped environment could turn the South Asian security equation into a question of fate rather than forethought.[59]

General Sundarji and US experts like Professor Kenneth N. Waltz contend that the nuclear status of all three nations, India, Pakistan, and China, lends itself towards tri-polar nuclear deterrence.[60] They further argue that this situation parallels US-Soviet bipolar deterrence during the Cold War. The fallacy of this thought process is fourfold. The first issue is that the US and Soviet Union have no common border. There was a smaller chance of open conflict erupting because of animosity at an adjacent border. Second, the US and Soviet Union never directly confronted each other but always through proxies. India has faced Pakistan and China on four separate occasions and has frequent encounters on each border. Third, neither India nor Pakistan has a second strike capability which is a potentially destabilizing situation because of the high payoff achievable by a first strike.[61] This capability, common to the US and USSR arsenals, provided a great stabilizing force as a nuclear equalizer and deterrent. Finally, India's antagonism with Pakistan goes beyond political or ideological issues and advances into cultural and religious hostilities. This deeper based hostility shortens the fuse for possible conflict and raises the stakes to national survival. At first, the discussion of multiple deterrence appears reasonable, but when examined in context, nuclear weapons within the region do not offer stability through deterrence but add to regional complexity.

---

59   Praful Bidwai, "India's Foreign Policy" *New Statesman & Society* 7 (July 94): 11.

60   "Arms Control in South Asia," 12.

61   Anderson, 127.

2.6 Future Prospects

Adding to the military variables within the region is a burgeoning arms race between China and India. Economics directly drives the acquisition of military capital, and, as noted previously, India has temporarily slowed its military budget in recent years while China has increased defense spending 26% between 1988 and 1995 to $24 billion.[62] However, in a RAND study titled "Long Term Economic and Military Trends, 1994-2015," K.C. Yeh and Anil Bamezai analyzed trends in both countries out to the year 2015. If economic liberalization continues for India, the authors postulated that India's gross domestic product (GDP) will rise from $1.2 trillion to $3.7 trillion in 2015. For China, two alternate scenarios were developed to reflect a stable China scenario and a disrupted growth scenario. From $5.0 trillion, China's GDP increases to $9.0 trillion in the unstable scenario and $13.6 trillion in a stable China scenario. Interestingly, when the authors studied the military capital of both countries, the differences were not that extreme. Yeh and Bamezai conclude that in the long term, "India's military capital rises substantially relative to that of China, reaching by 2015 about 77 percent of China's military capital in the stable-growth scenario, and slightly exceeding that of China in the second disrupted-growth scenario."[63] The RAND authors quickly note that uncertainties will affect their predictions, but their analysis does indicate that India will likely remain militarily relevant although not dominant within Asia.

---

[62]   Damon Bristow, "Mutual mistrust still hampering Sino-Indian rapprochment," *Jane's Intelligence Review* 9 no. 8 (August 1997): 371.

[63]   Charles Wolf, Jr., K.C. Yeh, Anil Bamezai, and others, *Long-Term Economic and Military Trends 1994-2015: The United States and Asia*, MR-627-OSD (Santa Monica, CA: The Rand Corp., 1995), 17.

2.7 Escalating Capabilities

India's increasing military capability is an expression of its direct and observable security needs as well as its desire for greater status in the region. Facing internal disorder as well as external dangers, the armed forces of India are a cultural outgrowth of India itself. With India's primary threats originating internally as well as from Pakistan and China, India's focus has been land oriented. Since the early 1970's, India has been improving its operational capabilities while moving towards a more dynamic force structure. With the success of high tech weapons demonstrated by the US in the Persian Gulf, Indian strategists have realized that "a state of technological asymmetry [is] the underlying factor for success" in future conflicts.[64] However, recent force modernization efforts have been hampered by an economic downturn and a constrained budget. India planners realize that its armed forces are currently inadequate to handle a dual war with its primary enemies: Pakistan and China. This has led India to adopt a nuclear and missile program which demonstrates a weapons capability without going to full production. It is through this calculated "capability" that India plans to maintain regional deterrence while simultaneously enjoying an elevated status within the world of nations. However, India's inferiority compared with China is not absolute, and as noted within a RAND study for 2015, "India may exercise a counterweight to China's apparent dominance" within the region.[65] The underlying currents within the Indian military denote a pattern of increased capabilities with a desire for power projection through nuclear development, missile technology, and aviation and naval procurements. However, the immaturity of the strategic planning process within the Indian government indicates the potential downside if these capabilities are used imprudently. The risk associated with these developments against a backdrop of accelerating Asian economic and

---

[64]   Nair, 97.

[65]   Wolf, preface xv.

23

military expansion is an increased potential for crisis within a region patterned with periodic clashes.

CHAPTER THREE
EXTERNAL RELATIONS

3.1 General

When India emerged at independence, it was significantly affected by the radically changed world order of post World War II. Consumed with feelings of victory after gaining independence from a weakened England in 1947, India attempted to chart a course that steered it away from taking sides in the developing ideological conflict between the US and the USSR.

With an extensive cultural heritage and a successful independence movement, India saw itself as an independent world leader and voice for populations that were dominated by colonial empires. This foreign policy orientation was a natural impulse to the anti-colonial resentment felt by many Indians and was the genesis of the Non-Aligned Movement (NAM) in 1956.[66] However, events would radically alter India's foreign policy direction. Successive wars with Pakistan and China, on again-off again relations with the US, and a growing dependence on the USSR for military and political support changed India's external orientation. Complicating the political dynamics of the Cold War era was the development of a substantial cultural and political conflict between India and Pakistan concurrent with the ideological conflict between the US and USSR. The regional diplomatic intrigues during this period were only matched by the shifting alliance structures as each of these four states

---

66   Thakur, 25.

maneuvered politically and sometimes militarily for a position of dominance within the region.[67]

The disintegration of the Soviet Union marked the end of this high profile struggle, but historical and regional animosities within South Asia still exist. The rules have changed. For India, the result has been a foreign policy that has been "unable to define an independent role or political space for itself."[68] Dependent on "the logic of the Cold War", Indian strategic policy runs counter to the nation's self interests.[69] The confused signals sent by India concerning the 1990-91 Gulf crisis portray this dilemma. Indian sympathy for Saddam Hussein and the limited support offered by India to the US-led coalition ran against India's need for stable oil prices and the employment opportunity for thousands of Indians generated by an independent Kuwait. By not vehemently opposing Iraq's actions, India contradicted all the principles that it had exposed in the NAM and the UN. As India contemplates its security concerns within a new international political paradigm, the country faces some serious foreign policy adjustments. To gain an understanding of developing external Indian behavior patterns, an examination of past Indian relations with Pakistan, the US, and China will outline possible directions for Indian foreign relations within a subregional and regional context.

---

[67] For more discussion concerning the diplomatic progression of post independent India see Dennis Kux, *Indian and the United States: Estranged Democracies?*

[68] Bidwai, 11.

[69] Dr. Thomas Thorton, Georgetown and Johns Hopkins Universities, *The Cold War Foundations*, a discussion paper presented at the 1997 India Symposium sponsored by the National Defense University at Ft. McNair, Washington, D.C. on 3 December 1997, 1.

3.2 Pakistan

The origins of conflict between India and Pakistan stretch back to partition in 1947. Indian Muslims, fearing a nationalist Hindu majority, petitioned Britain for the creation of a separate, Muslim state within the subcontinent. The petition gained credence as communal passions within the subcontinent flamed against the future of an independent India, and hundreds of thousands of Muslims, Hindus and Sikks were killed in widespread rioting. The outcome of partition left all parties dissatisfied. Indian nationalists saw a divided subcontinent robbed of the potential that former colonial India possessed. Additionally, the creation of Pakistan appeared to justify Muslim apprehensions towards a Hindu majority, insulted Indian nationalists who labored for a secular state, and became an open sore for civil stability in every Indian province with a sizable Muslim presence. Pakistan was now a country, but its "truncated" formation with an East and West Pakistan gave it strategic weakness.[70] The subcontinent that had been united politically through the conquests of the Moghul and British empires was now separated, and the subcontinent contended with two nations that were culturally linked but religiously and politically divided.

Complicating the partition problems was the question of Kashmir. Located at the juncture of the India, Pakistan, Afghanistan, and China frontiers, Kashmir's Hindu Maharaja elected to accede to the Indian Union while the majority of the population, which was Muslim, wanted Kashmir as a natural state within Pakistan. This conflict led directly to the first Indo-Pakistan war, which was settled by a UN cease-fire on 1 January 1949. However, UN negotiations did not solve the Kashmir problem as both sides reneged on conditions that they had agreed on, namely a popular vote to determine Kashmir's status and the withdrawal of Pakistani aid to insurgents. India followed with a military occupation of eastern Kashmir while Pakistan began to arm and train Kashmir insurgents in a war by proxy.

---

[70]   Rao, 32.

Kashmir presents strategists on both sides with serious dilemmas. On the Indian side, an independent or Pakistani Kashmir threatens national unity as other secession movements see opportunity.[71] Holding Kashmir by force is a drain on the national treasury, does not correspond with democratic government and is a source of insecurity with India's large Muslim minority (approximately 120 million). For Pakistan, Kashmir is symbol of Hindu hegemony and justifies the reason for Pakistan's creation. However, Kashmir is also a larger drain on Pakistan's more limited resources. In addition, Pakistan has its own secessionist problems that parallel the internal unity problems that India face. Indian funding of large militant groups within Pakistan (Sindhis and Baluchis) adds to destabilization as these groups have become more autonomous in terms of Indian control. Resolving the Kashmir crisis will likely provide neither side a clear and conclusive victory. No matter what the verdict, the question of Kashmir sovereignty will only add greater complexity to Indian politics.

Although Kashmir is the major symbol of conflict between India and Pakistan, the real issue for India is dominance of the subcontinent. The two countries have fought three wars that have resulted in neither side gaining a total victory. Pakistan's development of a substantial army challenges India's aspirations as the dominant subregional state because Pakistan can resist Indian political cohercion. In this light, Pakistan acts as the only other "sovereign" nation within the subcontinent when examined against the Indira Doctrine.[72] From the Indian viewpoint, the challenge posed by Pakistan offers a beacon of resistance for other South Asian nations to follow.

Pakistan's conventional armed forces are smaller when compared to India and do not challenge India's survival. Table two portrays relative personnel and organization strengths, but it fails to indicate that India provides a relatively sizeable force (mountain divisions plus significant air forces) to counter the China threat. In this light, Indian strategists consider

---

[71]   Thakur, 58.

[72]   Tanham, 31.

28

Armed Forces	Personnel	Armored Divisions	RAPID Divisions	Infantry Divisions	Mountain Divisions	Indep Brigades	Combat Aircraft
India	1,145,000	3.00	4.00	18.00	9.00	15.00	777.00
Pakistan	587,000	2.00	0.00	19.00	0.00	16.00	429.00

Table 2. Derived from *The Military Balance 1997/1998.* Edited by Col. Terence Taylor and published by Oxford University for the International Institute for Strategic Studies.

Pakistan a substantial South Asian threat. This is not only because of the sizeable forces that India must maintain against Pakistan, but it also stems from the extra-regional allies that Pakistan courts (US and China) who have contributed to Pakistan's disproportionately large military capability.

Pakistan's US relationship was born from the US containment policy against the Soviet Union. The relationship developed into a triangle as Pakistan appeared as a willing partner to the US while the US alienated India by supporting India's archrival. This three-way relationship moved up and down depending on the circumstances but reached two significant climaxes. The first, in 1971, occurred when India successfully split Pakistan with the creation of Bangladesh. The second occurred with the 1979 Soviet invasion of Afghanistan. With Pakistan now on the front-line of Soviet aggression, the US greatly increased its support to Pakistan. Pakistan exploited this series of events to increase its military capability and expand its nuclear research while India viewed Pakistani acquisition efforts as a threat. Fueling Indian fears and irritating Indian-US relations during the 1980's, Pakistan still deployed 80% of its military forces on the Indian vice the Afghanistan border as US support effectively strengthened Pakistan's position against India.[73]

The culmination of this deepening Indo-Pakistani rift was an Indian military exercise called Brass Tacks. Brass Tacks originated from Rajiv Gandhi at the end of 1985 as a symbolic gesture of Indian military power.[74] The exercise was conceived as a large scale

---

[73]   Thakur, 44.

[74]   Bajpai, 27.

29

troop and armor movement in response to a simulated Pakistani attack in Kashmir and took place in early 1987. Involving all three services and numerous government agencies, Brass Tacks was to serve as a test bed for mechanized forces and command and control systems at the army level. It was comparable to a large scale NATO or Warsaw Pact exercise.[75] Through a series of miscalculations and misjudgments, or as some contend by calculation and premeditation, the exercise devolved into a general crisis as Pakistani and Indian forces deployed in response to each other.[76] After serious brinkmanship to avert a crisis, some key lessons were learned. For the Pakistanis, the exercise served as another sign of Indian aggressiveness and irresponsible leadership. Furthermore, the exercise probably justified a greater drive to nuclear weapon development as Pakistan realized the US was not coming to its defense.[77] For the Indian government, the exercise displayed the "lack of institutional decision making" at the ministerial level and too much centralization of power by the Prime Minister.[78] The Indian military was also surprised by the capability and performance of the Pakistani forces during the crisis as compared to the 1971 conflict. This firm response by Pakistan was not expected and only added to Indian security fears.

The international triangle changed as the Soviets faced defeat in Afghanistan and withdrew in 1988. This resulted in a reevaluation of US policy regarding Pakistan. Subsequently, the US (Pressler amendment) blocked the sale of US F-16's and other military equipment to Pakistan because of fears of Pakistani nuclear weapon research and possible Pakistani nuclear proliferation. This changed US-Pakistan relations but did not change Pakistan's intentions to maintain strategic parity with India. This has been accomplished by

---

75   Bajpai, 3.

76   Bajpai, 4.

77   Bajpai, 92.

78   Bajpai, 43.

30

Pakistan's increased reliance on China to gain the military technology that it needs to support its missile and nuclear programs.[79] In addition, Pakistan continues its efforts against India by waging a proxy war in the regions of Punjab and Kashmir.[80]

Between India and Pakistan there have been many cases of conflict termination, but there has been no strategy for conflict resolution. This inherent inability to come to a peaceful solution resides in the partition process itself and the ensuing years of conflict. India's strategic options concerning Pakistan fall into a category of diametric opposition. The fear of losing Kashmir as a precursor to national dismemberment fuels debate within India while forcibly controlling Kashmir runs counter to the democratic principles that India was built.[81] Moreover, the resources that India uses to maintain a military against Pakistan are self-defeating because of Pakistani maneuvers to oppose Indian force buildups. Finally, the interjection of a third party like the US or China within the confines of the subcontinent compounds India's political difficulties. With a third party changing the regional balance and raising the strategic stakes, the underlying issues of the Indo-Pakistani conflict become more amplified. Pakistan as well as India needs an aggressive opponent for self-identity and its own stability. Pakistan and northern Indians share a common civilization in the form of food, music, language and culture.[82] If normalization were to occur, the reason for Pakistan's creation would come into question. Diametrically opposing each other, India and Pakistan cannot tolerate the other's existence within the subcontinent while simultaneously depending on each other for national identity and internal cohesion.

---

[79]   Willis Witter, "Christopher Sets Aside Differences, Boosts Ties," *The Washington Times*, 21 November 1996, Sec. A14.

[80]   Thakur, 54.

[81]   Raju G.C. Thomas, *India's Security Environment: Towards the Year 2000*, Monograph, Strategic Studies Institute (Carlisle Barracks, PA: January 1996), Sec III, 2.

[82]   Thakur, 62.

3.3 The United States

The US represents a significant variable to future Indian foreign policy directions because of its political influence and power projection capabilities within the region. Although the following discussion revolves around Indian-US relations, it is impossible for the US to manipulate lines of policy with one nation in the region without tugging on the interests of other actors in the immediate vicinity. US policy statements concerning the GOI are immediately read for context in Islamabad or Beijing. The same rules apply for New Delhi with US communications conducted with any of India's neighbors. For India, the US poses a considerable strategic dilemma. For some Indians, the US is a foreign threat with naval and air bases on Diego Garcia and has militarily bolstered India's neighbors and appears committed to global hegemony. For other Indians, the US is an economic necessity for India to lift its impoverished masses. An examination of this fluctuating relationship will provide insight on the possible future outcome of Indian-US relations.

From the US perspective, the most important stumbling block for Indian-US relations was India's relationship with the Soviet Union. Despite the US's economic importance as a major donor of bilateral aid from 1951 until 1971, this alienation was only accented by India's perception of the US's single minded stance against communism above all other US policy.[83] Indian leaders became increasingly irritated with the US as a meddling and intrusive influence because the US attached policy requirements to aid packages and restricted Indian weapons purchases from US vendors. India's ties with the Soviet Union were initially in concert with Prime Minister Nehru's Non-Aligned policy (1950's). The Chinese threat posed by India's defeat in the 1962 Border War only enhanced this relationship. Providing India a strategic ally against China, this fostering relationship had an even greater effect alienating Indian-US relations. In addition, the Indian government and

---

[83]   Kux, 448.

32

press has viewed American policy in the region as imperialistic. Contributing to this fear of US imperialism was the US agreement with the United Kingdom (December 1966) which made the islands of the British Indian Ocean Territory available for US defense purposes. The construction of a US naval and air facility beginning in early 1971 on Diego Garcia only supported this view. As Diego Garcia grew into a military forward staging base in the 1970's and 1980's, Indian fears of US military dominance grew. Amplifying Indian fears of US military dominance in the region was America's demonstration of military power during the Persian Gulf Crisis. The words of BrigGen V.K. Nair, former Deputy Director General for Strategic Planning, illustrate this fear: "From the word go, the behaviour pattern of the United States during the confrontation with Iraq [was] indicative of this super power's intentions to indulge its aspirations for global political and military hegemony."[84]

Another significant stumbling block from the Indian perspective has been the US-Pakistan relationship. By aligning with Pakistan and providing it with economic and military support, the US became linked with India's principal security threat. America's involvement with Pakistan beginning in the early 1950's as a part of the US containment policy against communism. This placed the US in a difficult position of supporting a military dictatorship with a history of repression. However, the cost of business with Pakistan was considered profitable when contrasted against the threat of the Soviet Union. This became especially apparent after the 1979 Soviet invasion of Afghanistan. Pakistan profited from the relationship because of the military support it received but more important the political value of a US relationship. This relationship soon changed as the Soviets withdrew from Afghanistan, and the US reconsidered its relations with Pakistan. The end of the Cold War diminished Pakistan's importance to US policy in the subregion except in the case of nuclear non-proliferation. Implementation of the Pressler Amendment and other economic

---

[84]   Nair, 201.

restrictions placed on Pakistan coupled with Pakistan's closer ties with China indicate the divergence of US-Pakistan mutual interest.

The diminishing significance of Pakistan improved Indian-US relations, and indicators support this position. American foreign investment in India is by far the largest of any nation.[85] The US has become India's largest trading partner and is a major supporter for India's acquisition of foreign credit.[86] However, some Indian resentments do exist. These resentments generate from Indian frustrations with US political intrusion as well as fears of neo-colonialism in the form of US investments as described in chapter one. US concerns for human rights in Kashmir and other areas of India, for Indian nuclear proliferation progress, and for Indian missile developments are just a few issues that the Indian government feels the US is overstepping its bounds.[87] Exemplifying this hostility are those within the External Affairs Ministry who see improved Sino-Indian relations as a counter to the military, economic and political dominance of the US.[88]

But India needs the US far more than the US needs India. With the loss of markets in the Soviet Union, which in turn cut markets in the Warsaw Pact, India had to shift economic emphasis to the US, making the US its largest trading partner. However, only 1.5 percent of US trade goes to India, placing it in a large category of countries in Asia that competes for US attention.[89] This places India, with a population rapidly approaching one billion, in an unenviable position as a peripheral US interest.

---

[85] Clad, 108.

[86] Thakur, 171.

[87] Swapan Dasgupta, "Clinton's Sanctimonious Diplomacy," *World Press Review 41* (June 1994): 50.

[88] Thomas, Sec III, 2.

[89] Clad, 113.

India appears embittered with the US because of its historical ties with Pakistan, its economic and military dominance in the region, and the "benign neglect" the US shows India.[90] These issues have combined to create a seesaw relationship since Indian independence. The pattern of misunderstandings and misconceptions concerning each country's role in the South Asia region is convoluted and steeped in emotion. This has diminished potential relations. The end of the Cold War and the emergence of a burgeoning China has marked a turning point for India-US relations. However, within the region, the US will likely continue its focus on the Chinese economy that is two and one half times larger ($3.5 trillion versus India's $1.4 trillion in 1994) and expanding at a higher rate.[91] India's concern with the US presence in the Indian Ocean (Diego Garcia) as well as the Persian Gulf will remain a volatile issue. This concern will add to India's insecurity for what it considers its maritime domain. Fundamental values such as economic prosperity, internal stability, peace and democracy for both India and the US are the same. The problem lies with the rapid pace of economic development within the Pacific Rim and China. This economic potential represents a source of trade and markets to the US while threatening to dwarf India's political and economic relevance in the region.

3.4 China

Although Indian strategists recognize Pakistan as the most immediate threat to security, "New Delhi believes that India has good reason to be concerned about China's long-term strategic intentions."[92] For some 2500 years, India and China coexisted peacefully.

---

[90]   Anderson, 132.

[91]   US Department of Commerce, International Trade Commission, "Economic Trends and Outlook for India," and "Economic Trends and Outlook for China," downloaded from the National Trade Data Bank and Economic Bulletin Board (Quantico, VA: Erols), 11 November 1997.

[92]   Montaperto, 5.

With the Himalayan watershed as the recognized border between the two ancient civilizations, the two "new" countries that emerged in the late 1940's appeared to have no reason to quarrel. However, it was not long before China and India engaged in combat over border disputes in the Himalayas. A discussion of the origins and issues of Sino-Indian relations will frame the future relations between the world's two most populous nations.

The challenge for Sino-Indian relations began in 1950 with the Chinese invasion of Tibet. Although Indian strategists were concerned, Prime Minister Nehru recognized the invasion in the 1954 Sino-Indian Agreement. His intent was to appease China and avoid alignment with the West. Contained within the preamble of the treaty were five principles for international tranquillity called *Panchsheel* : "respect for each other's integrity and sovereignty, mutual non-aggression, mutual noninterference in each other's internal affairs, equality and mutual benefit and peaceful coexistence."[93] Recognizing Tibet as an autonomous region of China, Indian leaders distanced themselves from the issue of Tibet independence. The Tibet revolt in 1959 and the resulting hundred thousand exiled Tibetans only accented the contrast between Indian policy and the realities of Chinese repression. However, the Dalai Lama, exiled leader of Tibet, brought out the flaw in Indian strategic thinking in an address in New Delhi in 1959.[94] If Tibet had no international standing as Indian policy alleged, then the agreement between Tibet and British India in the 1914 Simla convention, delineating India from Tibet, was nullified. This in turn negated the validity of the McMahon line that runs between Bhutan and Burma and all border claims made by British India with regard to China. The Dalai Lama's observation set the stage for the India-China Border War of 1962.

The border dispute involved three separate areas: the North East Frontier in the East, the Tibetan sector in the middle and the Ladakh sector in the West which borders Kashmir

---

[93]   Tanham, 36.

[94]   Thakur, 68.

and Jammu. These borders were drawn by the British in the early 20th century and reflected the British empire's strength at the time. The intent was to place the borders as far forward as possible to give the Indian subcontinent strategic depth. Because of poor mapping skills and the isolation of the area, the exact location of the border remained in doubt. In 1961, Nehru's government adopted a more aggressive position and started sending out patrols past Chinese positions with the mission of securing outposts in the Aksai Chin plateau. Control of this plateau would give the Indian government a more advantageous position diplomatically when the two governments met to discuss border settlements.[95] However, the Chinese considered the Aksai Chin road linking Tibet with Sinkiang strategically vital.[96] By 1962, the Chinese government started their own patrolling in the North East Frontier as a response to what they perceived as Indian aggression.

The Chinese were acclimatized and in a more advantageous military position on the Tibetan plateau to support military operations. By contrast, the Indians were in poor defensive positions with a limited road network to support their operations. Additionally, they were not acclimatized, equipped with winter clothing, or comparably armed. As the crisis developed, the Chinese mounted an attack along the entire border on 20 October 1962 with vastly superior numbers. Their mission was to gain ground to halt the Indian forward policy and to "humble and expose [India's] weakness."[97] Overwhelmed, the Indian government was in a state of panic. The situation appeared grave enough for Indian Prime Minister Nehru to forego his policy of "Non-Alignment" and ask for Western military support in the form of aircraft, radar equipment and other military equipment. After a brief but successful offensive operation, the Chinese announced a cease-fire on 20 November and

---

[95]   Kux, 202.

[96]   Rao, 391.

[97]   Tanham, 36.

began to consolidate their positions. Although the Indian government did not face a full scale military invasion, Chinese forces deftly handed India a military defeat and effectively generated a crisis of faith in its military capabilities. Indian leaders, namely Prime Minister Nehru, had miscalculated Chinese responses to the border incursions and greatly underestimated the strength of the Chinese military. The issue of the Border War has been the subject of numerous negotiations, and it is still a sore point in Sino-Indian relations. Indian diplomats have attempted to negotiate and compromise on a settlement, but both countries maintain considerable forces along the border poised against each other.

The final issue that has adversely affected Sino-Indian affairs has been India's relationship with the Soviet Union. India was initially attracted to the Soviet Union in the 1950's as a model for a planned self-sufficient economy and due to US expanding relations with Pakistan. The Soviet Union consolidated its strategic position with India after the 1962 Border War with China. With a common anti-China interest, the two naturally converged. Indian defense planners counted on large numbers of China's best troops to be deployed on the Soviet border. The Soviet Union looked to India as a counterweight to China from within the region and supplied it generously with military hardware. As this relationship deepened, India's alignment with the Soviet Union grew more close. Besides the 1971 Indo-Soviet Friendship Treaty described in chapter two, another indication of this close relationship was India's response after the Soviet invasion of Afghanistan in 1979. Western observers interpreted Indira Gandhi's weak protest as effectively support for the Soviet Union. India's hesitant position on this flagrant invasion of a non-aligned nation, considering India's normally strong position against such actions, can be explained in terms of its continuing need for Soviet support both politically and militarily to counter the China and Pakistan threat.

With Sino-Soviet relations warming in the late 1980's and the subsequent implosion of the Soviet Union, the northern threat to China disappeared. India's relative standing with China deteriorated without diplomatic or military support from the Soviet Union. This caused a change in Indian policy with several overtures made to the Chinese beginning in the 1980's and a state visit by Rajiv Gandhi in December 1988. Although talks have continued, the basic issues of Tibet and the border have remained unchanged. The Indian government has demonstrated its willingness to accommodate the Chinese by acknowledging Chinese authority over Tibet while limiting Tibetan protests in India. However, this appeasement policy has not won any diplomatic rewards, and the Chinese remain unmoved concerning disposition of the boundary dispute. Indian authorities privately acknowledge that the reason behind India's renewed diplomatic overtures with China is India's inability, given a reduced military budget, to fight two closely allied neighbors simultaneously.[98] Given the circumstances, the GOI wants the appearance of progress concerning the border issues with their public and touts the new accords signed in 1996 as evidence of continuing normalization. However, an examination of the documents demonstrates that the "new" accords are a reiteration of prior accords, and, although they improve other aspects of the relationship by increasing confidence between the two countries, the border dispute remains unresolved.[99] As the Indian government works to develop a plan to recover territory lost during the 1962 War (approximately 12,000 square miles of relatively valueless land), the country faces three conflicting issues that will complicate or impede normal relations with China. The first is an Indian ego which perceives a border compromise as submission to Chinese aggression. Running counter to this perception is an Indian government that cannot "afford" an increased military competition with its more prosperous neighbor while it is simultaneously working to expand its own economy. Lastly, the Tibet "problem" could become a major impediment to normalized relations if Tibetan expatriates in India increase their level of resistance to Chinese rule over Tibet. The situation would likely destabilize

---

98   Brahma Chellaney, "India, China Try To Overcome History of Mistrust," *The Washington Times*, 7 December 1996, Sec. A7.

99   Chellaney, Sec. A7.

Chinese control over Tibet, resulting in Chinese pressure on India to quell Tibetan protests and support. This would "rapidly become a political issue and an issue of Indian nationalism which would present any Indian government with a dilemma."[100]

Despite the warming trend that negotiations suggest, Indian strategists are alarmed that China has taken an expansionist role within Asia. Chinese support for Pakistan in the form of M-11 missiles, ring magnets for nuclear research, and general military equipment gives Indian planners plenty to worry about in the sub-region. China does not have to qualify its relationship with Pakistan to improve relations with India because India needs a peaceful China. Pakistan also enhances China's bargaining position with India while acting as China's agent to the Islamic world. China has the best of both worlds as it negotiates down to India, treating it on the same level as Pakistan.[101]

Amplifying Indian feelings of encirclement are Chinese relations with Myanmar or Burma. Since the State Law and Order Restoration Council (SLORC) took control of the government in 1988, it has embraced Chinese economic and military support. China has been well positioned economically with Burma, and trade between the two nations has increased to over $1.5 billion dollars a year.[102] China enjoys a near monopoly with Burmese infrastructure construction, but, what is more important, Burma has imported approximately $1.5 billion dollars worth of military equipment from China.[103] This military equipment is also supported by Chinese instructors. These factors coupled with reports of a naval radar facility on Great Coco Island and the planned construction of a deep water port

---

100   Montaperto, 6.

101   Chellaney, Sec. A7.

102   Andrew Selth, "Burma and the Strategic Competition between China and India," *The Journal of Strategic Studies* 19, no.2 (June 1996): 214.

103   Selth, 215.

on Hainggyi Island to support the Chinese navy magnify Indian fears of Chinese encroachment.

Chinese animosity to Taiwan, a crackdown in Tibet, and evidence that China is lengthening runways at eleven air force bases in Tibet also causes concern in New Delhi.[104] This concern has been echoed by the former chiefs of the Indian armed forces who urged the Indian Congress in early 1996 to support increases in military spending and to concentrate on blocking China's long term plans in the South Asian subregion.[105] Supporting Indian military apprehension is a Chinese strategist's term referring to the need for "survival space" *(shengcun kongjian)* and for "strategic frontiers that extend horizontally into the Indian Ocean."[106] Bolstering this strategic concept, the Chinese have made a significant increase in naval spending in the 1990's that parallels the rapid growth of the Indian navy in the 1980's except on a larger scale.[107]

The strategic implication for China is to maintain the course that has already been set. Political and military cooperation with Pakistan and Burma, combined with an unyielding attitude concerning border negotiations suit China well. Although Chinese policies may not be designed with a purpose of keeping India off balance and focused on the periphery, their net overall impact has this effect. Chinese vital interests relate directly to its overriding priority for economic development which include access to Southeast Asian markets as well as access to petroleum from the Middle East and future oil reserves in Central Asia.[108] Dr.

---

[104]   Bristow, 370.

[105]   Thomas, Sec. III, 2.

[106]   Samuel S. Kim, *China's Quest for Security in the Post-Cold War World*, Monograph, Strategic Studies Institute (Army War College: April 1996), Chapter I-4.

[107]   Thomas, Sec. III, 2.

[108]   Michael Lelyveld, "Greater Asian role seen in Persian Gulf, Caspian Sea," *Journal of Commerce*, 12 Nov 97, 20.

Ronald Montaperto from the Institute for National Strategic Studies at the National Defense Univeristy comments that "the Indian interface with China in Southeast Asia may well mark a major fault line within the Asia Pacific region as two large and populous nations seek to achieve what each considers to be vital national interests."[109]

---

[109]   Montaperto, 6.

CHAPTER FOUR

INDIA'S STRATEGIC PROGNOSIS

4.1 Anticipating the Future

Long term Indian policies are difficult to discern. Plagued with internal political and ethnic fragmentation and an economy partially tethered to the past, Indian policy makers have a difficult balancing act to maintain. In this condition, the Indian military will likely attain a greater role within Indian society as it is seen as the cohesive force that preserves the union. Externally, India faces an even greater challenge. By placating China with envoys and "treaty" events, India looks to a future that offers a closer economic and political parity with China. However, this future depends on trading "time" for strategic "space" with China, as India labors to expand its recently liberated economy. This goal appears difficult to accomplish as India works to maintain subregional dominance while locked in a bitter embrace with Pakistan. Damon Bristow's comments in *Jane's Intelligence Review* illustrate the evolving India-China relationship:

> ... only the most optimistic observer would predict that the relationship between India and China will develop into anything more than a guarded friendship. Quite simply, India continues to view China with suspicion, believing that it is doing everything it can to frustrate India's ambitions in South Asia and beyond. China, meanwhile, remains aware that as India develops economically it will become a greater threat, both military and politically...[110]

However, India will not likely enter the 21st century on the heels of China's economy but at its feet. This situation will only inflame Indian elites as they watch China grow more economically dominant, engulf surrounding markets including Southeast Asia, and increase their military presence in the Indian Ocean. As this situation develops, India will resist this

---

[110]   Bristow, 371.

intrusion against what it believes as its domain in order to protect Indian sensitivities and to vent its frustration as a "near" great power.

Compounding India's problems is the existence of a well defined and immediate threat in the form of Pakistan. While creating a conventional security demand for India, Pakistan is one part of a convoluted regional nuclear stand off as well as an executor for Chinese interests. Dependent on each other, at least for the near term, for national identity, an Indo-Pakistan interaction increases the possibility for nuclear confrontation. Without the long established and transparent measures that existed within the US and USSR nuclear standoff, discussions of South Asian nuclear deterrence tend to minimize the real nuclear threat that exists in this region. Conflict resolution between Pakistan and India, while not impossible, remains doubtful within the bounds of the "Kashmir" problem and the historical animosity that exists between the two states.

How India interacts externally will depend on the capabilities at its disposal. While the Indian economy is not likely to match China's, the Indian military could offer a recalcitrant Indian government the only means to flex Indian influence within the region as well as a means of diverting attention away from its own internal problems. With an eye on technology, Indian military leaders have learned from US experience in the Persian Gulf. Strategically, the military is developing the capability to project landward and maritime power. Expanded missile programs and an undeclared nuclear weapon capability give India the veneer of world power status, but this craving for prestige brings an unhealthy variable within the environment. With the maturity of the Indian national security affairs apparatus in question, the ability of Indian strategists to analyze and process strategic implications and outcomes for a more fluid 21st century environment remains in doubt.

Adding a "wildcard" to the Asian strategic process, the US will remain, for the near term, a perplexing problem for Indian strategists to fathom. Strategic opportunities for India posed by closer ties with the US to counterbalance China remain currently unachievable because of political and economic disparities between the world's two largest democracies.

44

With an oscillating relationship, marked by a suspicious India and an economically ambivalent US, improved relations will not likely occur unless China overtly threatens the US and Asian stability. This places the US in an awkward diplomatic position of balancing on two "fences" between India and China as the possibility of a China-India confrontation looms on the horizon. On one side, the US must pursue a cautious and non-confrontational path with China in its efforts to maintain a policy of engagement and to assure penetration into a potentially lucrative market for the US economy. Simultaneously, the US must balance an Indian relationship that is not economically inviting but which could have potential security ramifications. Navigating this balance while preventing an India-China confrontation will be one of the difficult problems for US policy efforts in the next century.

4.2 Where to next?

The solution to this 21st century problem does not lie directly between India and China, but indirectly through India, Pakistan and the US. While China encroaches on India from Pakistan and the Indian Ocean, the probability of crisis climbs if China overextends its reach into one these two areas. Contemplating these possible "China" crises, New Delhi's range of solutions shrinks as it contends with Pakistan and other internal variables. If the US wants to prevent a greater regional confrontation, it must aggressively address the subregional issues between India and Pakistan. By promoting the transition to market economies for South Asia, the US could foster greater political stability while increasing the interaction between India and Pakistan at both the highest government levels and lowest business levels. The next step would be to integrate India and its neighbors into bilateral relationships with individual Asian countries beyond the ongoing dialogue in forums such as the Association of Southeast Asian Nations (ASEAN). By creating a positive atmosphere for conflict resolution through a combination of diplomatic and economic incentives for both parties, the US could surreptitiously neutralize China's advantage over India while working to minimize the possibility of an India-Pakistan nuclear confrontation. Although improved

45

relations between India and Pakistan remain in doubt, US action will buy "time" for economic expansion and diplomatic action which will provide "space" for India to improve its situation. The consequences of this action will determine whether India strides into the next century or collides with it.

BIBLIOGRAPHY

Adhikari, Gautam. *Sleeping with the Enemy: Problems of Economic Security in South Asia.* Discussion paper. Presented at the 1997 India Symposium sponsored by the National Defense University. Washington, DC: 3 December 1997.

Anderson, Nancy, Col, USMC and Jed Snyder, "India and Pakistan." Chapter 10 in *Strategic Assessment 1997: Flashpoints and Force Structure.* Eds. Hans A. Binnendijkand Patrick Clawson. Institute for National Strategic Studies. Washington DC: Ft. McNair, 1997.

"Arms Control in South Asia." downloaded from the *Journal of the Federation of American Scientists* Vol. 47, March/April 1994 (Quantico, VA: Erols), 15 September 1997.

Bajpai, Kanti P. and others. *BrassTacks and Beyond.* New Delhi: Manohar Pub., 1995.

Bidwai, Praful. "India's Foreign Policy" *New Statesman & Society* No. 7 (July 1994): 11.

Bristow, Damon. "Mutual mistrust still hampering Sino-Indian rapprochment." *Jane's Intelligence Review* 9 no. 8 (August 1997): 368-371.

Chellaney, Brahma. "India, China Try To Overcome History of Mistrust." *The Washington Times,* 7 December 1996, Sec. A7.

Clad, James, C. "India in 1996: Steady as She Goes." *The Washington Quarterly 19, no. 4* (Autumn 1996): 103-114.

Cohen, William S., US Secretary of Defense. Speech during an Asia Society conference on 6 June 1997. Downloaded from DefenseLINK News. Quantico, VA: Erols, 24 November 1997.

Cooper, Kenneth J. "With Door to Economy Ajar, India Can't Stop Shivering." *Washington Post,* 19 September 1997, Sec. A16.

Cox, Robert, D., MAJ., USA. *India and the Operational Art of War.* Monograph. U.S. Army Command and General Staff College, School of Advanced Military Studies. Ft. Leavenworth, KS: 1991.

Dasgupta, Swapan. "Clinton's Sanctimonious Diplomacy." *World Press Review 41* (June 1994): 50-51.

Dash, Kishore, C. "The Political Economy of Regional Cooperation in South Asia." *Pacific Affairs 69, no. 2* (Summer 1996): 185-209.

"Exploring U.S. Missile Defense Requirements in 2010: What are the Policy and Technology Challenges?," Institute for Foreign Policy Analysis Inc., April 1997. Downloaded from Federation of American Scientists: Missile Defense Monitor. Quantico, VA: Erols, 15 September 1997. Chapter 4.

Frankel, Francine. "Indo-U.S. Relations: The Future is Now." *The Washington Quarterly* 19, no. 4 (Autumn 1996): 129-148.

Harned, Glenn M., COL, USA. *The Complexity of War: The Application of Nonlinear Science to Military Science*. Monograph. Marine Corps War College. Quantico, VA: June 1995.

Kennedy, Paul. *Preparing For The Twenty-First Century*. New York: Vintage Books, 1994.

Kim, Samuel S. *China's Quest for Security in the Post-Cold War World*. Monograph. Strategic Studies Institute. Carlisle Barracks, PA: April 1996.

Kohli, Atul. "Can the Periphery Control the Center? Indian Politics at the Crossroads." *The Washington Quarterly 19, no. 4* (Autumn 1996): 115-127.

Kohli, S.N., Adm, PVSM, AVSM. "The geopolitical and strategic considerations that necessitate the expansion and modernization of the Indian Navy." *Indian Defence Review* 2 (January 1989): 33-46.

Krulak, Charles, Gen., USMC. "Protecting the Asian Promise." *Strategic Review 24, no. 3* (Summer 1996): 7-11.

Kux, Dennis. *India and the United States: Estranged Democracies 1941-1991*. Washington, DC: National Defense University Press, 1993.

Lacy, James, L. *Cautious Peace: Strategy and Circumstance In Asia-Pacific Security*. Monograph No. P-3108. Institute for Defense Analyses. Alexandria, VA: 1995.

Lelyveld, Michael. "Greater Asian role seen in Persian Gulf, Caspian Sea." *Journal of Commerce* (12 Nov 1997): 20.

Leonhard, Robert. *The Art of Maneuver*. Novato, CA: Presidio Press, 1991.

LePoer, Barbara, Leitch. *India - US Relations*, No. 93097. Downloaded from the Congressional Research Service Issue Brief: Foreign Affairs and National Defense Division. Quantico, VA: Erols, 9 December 1996.

Lewin, Roger. *Complexity, Life at the Edge of Chaos*. New York: Collier Books, 1992.

Mattoo, Amitabh. "India's Nuclear Status Quo." *Survival: The IISS Quarterly 38, no. 3* (Autumn 1996): 41-57.

Montaperto, Ronald N., Dr. *Emerging Dynamics of Indian Policy: A View from the United States*. Discussion paper. Presented at the 1997 India Symposium sponsored by the National Defense University. Washington, DC: 3 December 1997.

Nair, V.K., BrigGen., VSM (Ret.). War in the Gulf: Lessons for the Third World. New Delhi: Lancer Pub., 1991.

Nault, William J., Lt., USN. *The Strategic Impact Upon the United States of Future Naval Rivalries in South and Southeast Asia*. Monograph. Naval Postgraduate School. Monterey, CA: December 1992.

Perry, Floyd, L., COL., USA. *The Future of U.S. - India Relations*. Monograph. US Army War College. Carlisle Barracks, PA: 1991.

Rao, K.V. Krishna, Gen, PVSM (ret.). *Prepare or Perish: A Study of National Security.* New Delhi: Lancer Pub., 1991.

Scudieri, James, D., MAJ., USA. *The Indian Peace-Keeping Force in Sri Lanka, 1987-90.* Monograph. School of Advanced Military Studies, US Army Command and General Staff College. Ft. Leavenworth, KS: December 1994.

Selth, Andrew. "Burma and the Strategic Competition between China and India." *The Journal of Strategic Studies 19, no.2* (June 1996): 211-230.

Shridhar, D., Dr. "Testing Times Ahead for Indian Air Force." *Asia-Pacific Defence Reporter*. September-October, 1996, 13-14.

"Sonia's Choice." *The Economist.* 31 January 1998, 43.

Stremlau, John. "Dateline Bangalore: Third World Technopolis." *Foreign Policy* no. 102 (Spring 1996): 152-168.

Taylor, Terence, Col., ed. *The Military Balance 1997-98*. The International Institute for Strategic Studies. London: Oxford University Press, 1997.

Tanham, George K. *Indian Strategic Thought: An Interpretive Essay*. R-4207-USDP. Santa Monica, CA: The Rand Corp., 1992.

Thakur, Ramesh. *The Politics and Economics of India's Foreign Policy*. New York: St. Martin's Press, 1994.

Thomas, Raju, G. C. *India's Security Environment: Towards the Year 2000*. Monograph. Strategic Studies Institute. Carlisle Barracks, PA: January 1996.

Thorton, Thomas, Dr. *The Cold War Foundations.* Discussion paper. Presented at the 1997 India Symposium sponsored by the National Defense University. Washington, DC: 3 December 1997.

U.S. Department of Commerce, International Trade Commission. "Economic Trends and Outlook for India," and "Economic Trends and Outlook for China." Downloaded from the National Trade Data Bank and Economic Bulletin Board. Quantico, VA: Erols, 11 November 1997.

Waldrop, Mitchell M. *Complexity: The Emerging Science at the Edge of Order and Chaos.* New York: Simon and Schuster, 1992.

Witter, Willis. "Christopher Sets Aside Differences, Boosts Ties." *The Washington Times,* 21 November 1996, Sec. A-14.

Wolf, Charles, Jr., K.C. Yeh, Anil Bamezai, and others. *Long-Term Economic and Military Trends 1994-2015: The United States and Asia.* MR-627-OSD. Santa Monica, CA: The Rand Corp., 1995.